Must Know Sight Words Activity's Workbook

Dolch 1sr Grade

this book belongs to:

_____

- -

_____

Dolch Sight Words
1st Grade

after	from	know	round
again	give	let	some
an	going	live	stop
any	had	may	take
as	has	of	thank
ask	her	old	them
by	him	once	then
could	his	open	think
every	how	over	walk
fly	just	put	were
			when

How to use this workbook:

1.   Color inside the sight word.
2.   With a marker or dot-marker find all the sight words and say the word out-laud every time you find one.
3.   Count how many words you find and write the number on the star!

Complete the page by filing each exercise.

Color, cut and tape around your wrist to help you remember it throughout the day.

And most important: HAVE FUN!

Name:_____

Color and find the words!

every   after   stop   after

after   open   just   after

again   could   as

after   had   after

fly   give   after

by   ask

after

after

know

then   her   his

after   **after**

going   from   by   after

after   **an**

after   again   how   after

how many?

Name:_____

Sight Words Work

 Read It!

after

Write It!

Clap It!

① ② ③

Color It!

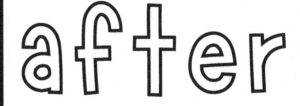

after

Trace It!

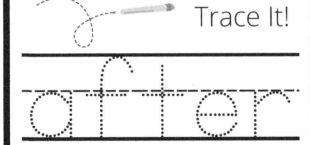

Spell It!

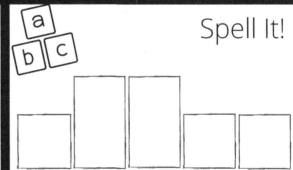

Fluency Sentence!

I run after the ball.

Name:_____

Color and find the words!

again   fly   may   stop | again |

live   again   just   again

again   again   as

of   had   again

again

by   again   ask

again   his   again

her   know

once   over   again

again   again   put

let

some   open

an   how many?

again

again   how   again

Name:_____

Sight Words Work

Read It!

again

Write It!

- - - - - - - - - - - - - -

Clap It!

① ② ③

Color It!

again

Trace It!

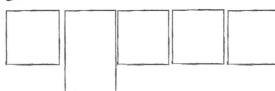
Spell It!

☐ ☐ ☐ ☐ ☐

Fluency Sentence!

Can I have ice cream again ?

Name:_____

Color and find the words!

an

any   an   may   an

live   give   just   going

an

an   as   an

of   had

form   **an**   an

an

ask

fly   **an**   her   an   him

an

an   how   **over**   ask

an   open   **an**   an

some   an   let

an   by   how   an

how many?

Name:_____

Sight Words Work

Read It!

an

Write It!

- - - - - - - - - -

Clap It!

(1) (2) (3)

Color It!

an

Trace It!

ᴀn

Spell It!

a
b c

[ ] [ ]

Fluency Sentence!

I saw an apple falling down.

Name:_____

Color and find the words!

any

could

any

every

any

live

any

as

any

from

give

any

just

any

had

him

any

let

ask

fly

any

her

any

any

how

any

ask

going

her

some

had

any

let

any

by

how

any

how many?

Name:_____

Sight Words Work

 Read It!

any

 Write It!

Clap It!

① ② ③

Color It!

any

 Trace It!

any

 Spell It!

☐ ☐ ☐

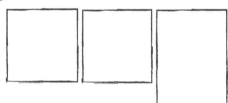

Fluency Sentence!

You can have any dog.

Name:_____

Color and find the words!

as   as
     could   every   as

live   as   as
     any

          from

     as   just   as   had

give

          let

     as   as

her   every

fly   as

     as   any   by   any

          how   ask

     as   going   as

some   had   as
          let

any   as   how   any

how many?

Name:_____

Sight Words Work

Read It!

as

Write It!

Clap It!

1 2 3

Color It!

as

Trace It!

as

Spell It!

a
b c

Fluency Sentence!

I am as happy as a clam.

Name:_____

Color and find the words!

ask

let   ask   know

ask

just

ask   any   his   him

how   has   ask

ask   had

ask

let

had

ask   her   ask   going

from   by   any

ask   going

fly   ask   give

some   ask   every   let

thank

ask   how   ask   how many?

Name:_____

Sight Words Work

Read It!

ask

Write It!

Clap It!

1 2 3

Color It!

ask

Trace It!

ask

Spell It!

a
b c

Fluency Sentence!

We ask mom for a bike.

Name:_____

Color and find the words!

by   live   know

by

old

may   by   his   by

once

by   of   by   had

let

open

any

by

by

by

how

going

over   by

by

from

some

put

by

fly

round

by

by   every

by

let

then

how many?

by   how   by

Sight Words Work

Name: _____

Read It!
by

Write It!

Clap It!
1 2 3

Color It!
by

Trace It!
by

Spell It!

Fluency Sentence!

I see the pig by the pen.

Color and find the words!

had   could   know   could

old

may   after   could   by

could   of   again   had

could

open   **could**

could

by   an   could   let

could   as   by

from   put   could

fly   round   ask

could   any   let

could

as   how   could   how many?

Name:_____

Sight Words Work

Read It!

could

Write It!

Clap It!

1 2 3

Color It!

could

Trace It!

could

Spell It!

Fluency Sentence!

Could **you pass me the hat.**

Color and find the words!

every

had   every   know   every

old

may

every

after   of   every   had

open   fly

every

every   an   every   let

from   every   by

from   every   every

put

fly   every   round   ask

any

every   let

every

as   how   every   how many?

Name:_____

Sight Words Work

 Read It!

every

 Write It!

Clap It!

① ② ③

Color It!

every

 Trace It!

every

 Spell It!

☐ ☐ ☐ ☐ ☐

Fluency Sentence!

I like to swim every day.

Color and find the words!

fly

fly give some fly

fly may

going fly

fly round

over fly had her

fly fly

once him

fly fly

old how

let take just fly

of fly live

stop round know

fly fly how many?

Name:_____

Sight Words Work

 **fly** Read It!

Write It!

Clap It!

① ② ③

Color It!

fly

Trace It!

fly

Spell It!

a
b c

Fluency Sentence!

We can fly on a jet.

Name:_____

Color and find the words!

from   give   **some**   from

from

may   round   **going**   from

from   him   again   had   her

from

from

from   ask   from

once

    by   over

old   how

    let   **know**

      take   from

of

    from   live

from

take   know

as   from

how many?

Name:_____

Sight Words Work

 Read It!

from

Write It!

Clap It!

(1) (2) (3)

Color It!

Trace It!

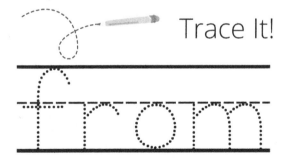

Spell It!

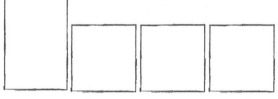

Fluency Sentence!

Where are you from ?

Color and find the words!

give

let   give   some   give

just

may   give   going   know

round   give   give   had

give

give

him   give

by

give   over   give

how

give   let   take   has

old   give

live

from   give

know

give   stop   from

how many?

Name:_____

Sight Words Work

Read It!

give

Write It!

Clap It!

1 2 3

Color It!

give

Trace It!

give

Spell It!

a
b c

Fluency Sentence!

Can I give you a hug?

Color and find the words!

going   could   some   going

just

may   going   know

how

round

going   him   fly   had   going

going

going   has

let   take   going   how

going

going   has   going

old   live

her

from   may   know

going   going   how many?

Name:_____

Sight Words Work

Read It!

going

Write It!

Clap It!

(1) (2) (3)

Color It!

going

Trace It!

going

Spell It!

Fluency Sentence!

We are going to the beach.

Name:_____

Color and find the words!

when   could   had | had |

just

had   had

round   live   had

how

fly   had   were

had

had   put

may   had

let   had   walk   how

had

of   has   open

had   had

then

from   had   had

think   once

how many?

Name:_____

Sight Words Work

 Read It!

had

Write It!

- - - - - - - - - - - - - - - -

Clap It!

(1) (2) (3)

Color It!

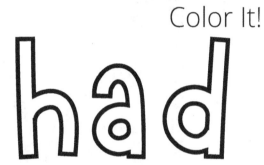

 **Trace It!**

Spell It!

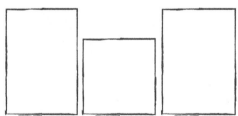

Fluency Sentence!

My dog had new pups.

Name:_____

Color and find the words!

has   could   has   [has]

just

has   has

round   live

fly   has   how

were   put

has

has

may   let   has   walk   how

has

of   had   has   has

how

then

from   has   has

think   once

how many?

Name:_____

Sight Words Work

Read It!

has

Write It!

Clap It!

1 2 3

Color It!

has

Trace It!

has

Spell It!

Fluency Sentence!

He has three pens

Name:_____

Color and find the words!

her   could   ask

her

her

after   every

her   live   her

how

fly   just   her   put

her

by   fly

her   her

let   her   walk

give

from   had   an   her

her

her

from   some   after

her   her

how many?

Name:_____

Sight Words Work

 Read It!

her

 Write It!

Clap It!

(1) (2) (3)

Color It!

her

 Trace It!

her

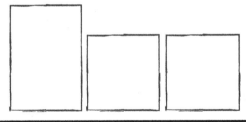 Spell It!

Fluency Sentence!

Her dad plays with us.

Name:_____

Color and find the words!

him   could   take | him |

him

round   every

him   live

him   how   him

fly   **him**   put

him

him

some   old

let   him   walk

give

from   had   once   him

him

him

from

when   after

him   him

how many?

Name:_____

Sight Words Work

 Read It!

him

Write It!

- - - - - - - - - - - - - - -

Clap It!

(1) (2) (3)

Color It!

him

Trace It!

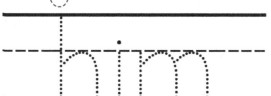

Spell It!

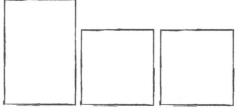

Fluency Sentence!

I give him a high five.

Name:_____

Color and find the words!

after   his   take | his |

round   his

avery   live   every

his   how   by

his

let   put

his   his

some   old

his   walk

his

from   going   his   from

give

his

from   know   after

his   his

how many?

Name:_____

Sight Words Work

 Read It!

his

 Write It!

Clap It!

1 2 3

Color It!

his

Trace It!

his

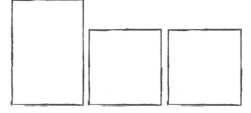 Spell It!

Fluency Sentence!

This is his yellow house.

Name:_____

Color and find the words!

after   how   **take**

how

every   round   every

live

how   how   how   by

put

let   how

how

old

how   walk

some

how   from   going   **how**   from

give

how   how

had   how

know   let

how many?

Name:_____

Sight Words Work

Read It!

how

Write It!

- - - - - - - - - -

Clap It!

① ② ③

Color It!

how

Trace It!

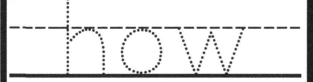

Spell It!

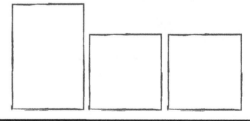

Fluency Sentence!

Show me how **it works.**

Color and find the words!

just   how   just   just

ask   just   how   just

how   how   live   how   by

let   just   just

some   just   walk   old

just   from   just   how   just

give

how   could   how

ask   just   how many?

just   just

Name:_____

Sight Words Work

Read It!
just

Write It!

Clap It!
1 2 3

Color It!
just

Trace It!
just

Spell It!

Fluency Sentence!

The blue car just left.

Color and find the words!

again   know   **stop**   know

ask   give   how   know

know

know   how   how   by

know

know

know

know   old

some   walk

know   from   **how**   know

know   how

how   how

let   from

know   know

how many?

Name:_____

Sight Words Work

Read It!

know

Write It!

Clap It!

(1) (2) (3)

Color It!

know

Trace It!

know

Spell It!

Fluency Sentence!

Do you know the answer?

Name:_____

Color and find the words!

every let just

let

give from let as

let any

her ask let let

let him

fly let

some old

let let

from how let

going just

let how

let let

after again how many?

Name:_____

Sight Words Work

Read It!

let

Write It!

Clap It!

1 2 3

Color It!

let

Trace It!

let

Spell It!

Fluency Sentence!

Can you let me have a pet?

Color and find the words!

live   may   just | live |

take   live   live

of   ask   any

                              her
stop   ask   live   live

live

them   **live**

live   over   old

put   live   from   how

take

once   **live**   live   round   live

old   how

live   live

after   *again*   how many?

Name:_____

Sight Words Work

 Read It!

live

Write It!

Clap It!

(1) (2) (3)

Color It!

Trace It!

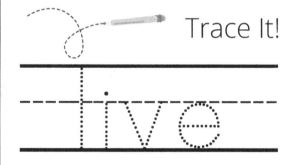

Spell It!

Fluency Sentence!

I live in the ocean, said the fish.

Name:_____

Color and find the words!

once   may   just   **may**

             open   may

put   ask   any

         may

               may   her   may

may   over

may

                                         of

thank   may

                                     may

may   from   **take**

                         may

round   live

         may   some

    then

may   how

    may   may   how many?

after   again

Name:_____

Sight Words Work

Read It!

may

Write It!

Clap It!

① ② ③

Color It!

may

Trace It!

may

Spell It!

Fluency Sentence!

May I have a snack please?

Color and find the words!

of   of

of

may

of

open   his

of

put

of

her   from

how

of

over

of

of

of

of

of

thank

take

of

ask

every

of

round

of

some

just

of

how

know

let

how many?

of

of

Name:_____

Sight Words Work

 Read It!

of

 Write It!

Clap It!

(1) (2) (3)

Color It!

 Trace It!

of

 Spell It!

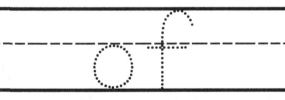

Fluency Sentence!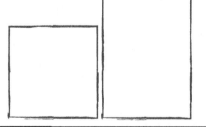

Today is the 1st day of June.

Color and find the words!

old

going

old

old

of

old

round

old

put

old

were

some

old

open

old

old

walk

stop

old

old

old

them

old

take

once

old

then

old

think

just

old

how

old

know

old

old

old

how many?

Name:_____

Sight Words Work

Read It!

old

Write It!

Clap It!

1 2 3

Color It!

old

Trace It!

old

Spell It!

Fluency Sentence!

I am 7 years old today.

Name:_____

Color and find the words!

over　　　　　round　　　| once |

　　once

some　　　round　　once　　thank

　　once　　　　once　　some　　once

open　　stop　　　　once　　walk

once

　　　　　　　　　　　　once
once　　fly　　once　　could

once　　then　　　　　by

just　　once　　going　　once

give　　once　　had　　once　　how many?

Name:_____

Sight Words Work

 Read It!

once

 Write It!

Clap It!

① ② ③

Color It!

once

 Trace It!

once

Spell It!

Fluency Sentence!

I saw a red fox once.

Name:_____

Color and find the words!

open

could

open

open

some

round

walk

open

open

open

some

then

open

stop

them

open

open

open

could

open

stop

by

once

then

open

open

old

open

of

how many?

open

open

give

had

Name:_____

Sight Words Work

 Read It!

open

Write It!

- - - - - - - - - - - - - - -

Clap It!

(1) (2) (3)

Color It!

Trace It!

Spell It!

Fluency Sentence!

Can you open **the jar please?**

Name:_____

Color and find the words!

over

ask

over

over

every

round

walk

over

over

over

then

let

over

her

over

over

over

them

could

over

over

put

any

over

may

round

over

over

of

over

walk

over

live

take

how many?

Name:_____

Sight Words Work

 Read It!

over

 Write It!

_____
- - - - - - - - - - - - - - -
_____

Clap It!

① ② ③

Color It!

over

 Trace It!

_____
over

 Spell It!

☐ ☐ ☐ ☐

Fluency Sentence!

We walk over the bridge.

Color and find the words!

after

put

over

put

every

put

put

round

put

from

let

her

put

put

them

put

her

put

p**ut**

could

may

put

put

any

round

put

put

put

of

put

when

put

take

walk

how many?

Name:_____

Sight Words Work

 Read It!

put

Write It!

Clap It!

① ② ③

Color It!

put

Trace It!

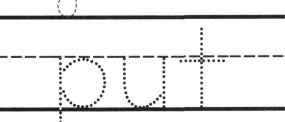

 Spell It!

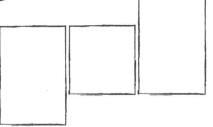

Fluency Sentence!

Where did I put my ball?

Color and find the words!

round

ask

round

round

every

after

of

round

round

round

let

her

put

some

round

open

round

could

round

round

put

round

any

put

round

know

how

round

of

take

his

round

how many?

walk

Name:_____

Sight Words Work

Read It!

round

Write It!

Clap It!

① ② ③

Color It!

round

Trace It!

round

Spell It!

Fluency Sentence!

My dad wears round glasses.

Name:_____

Color and find the words!

some

ask

some

some

every

some

some

after

some

some

let

her

put

live

open

some

some

some

some

put

old

any

some

some

some

take

of

thank

some

some

some

some

walk

how many?

Name:_____

Sight Words Work

 Read It!

some

 Write It!

- - - - - - - - - - - - - - - - -

Clap It!

(1) (2) (3)

Color It!

some

 Trace It!

 Spell It!

Fluency Sentence!

Can I have some cookies?

Name:_____

Color and find the words!

stop   stop   stop

open

live   after   of

stop

when

may   stop   were

walk   old

stop   stop   stop

stop

how   stop   old   stop

then   take

stop   stop

put   stop

think   stop   has   how many?

walk

Name:_____

Sight Words Work

 Read It!

stop

Write It!

Clap It!

① ② ③

Color It!

Trace It!

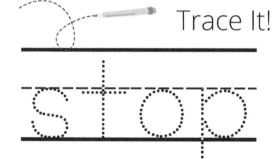

Spell It!

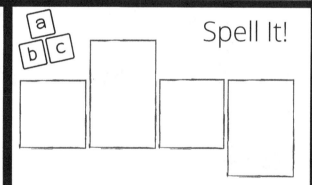

Fluency Sentence!

The stop sign is big and red.

Name:_____

Color and find the words!

take

open

every

take

live

again

take

after

take

take

take

then

take

were

an

take

old

take

could

old

take

take

then

old

just

let

take

take

know

take

her

has

how many?

take

Name:_____

Sight Words Work

 Read It!

take

 Write It!

_____
- - - - - - - - - - - - - - -
_____

Clap It!

(1) (2) (3)

Color It!

take

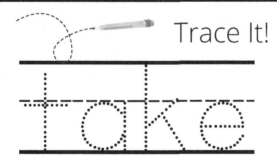 Trace It!

take

 Spell It!

Fluency Sentence!

Can I take my bear with me?

Name:_____

Color and find the words!

take   thank | take |

open

thank   take

after   again   thank

take   thank   were

take   old

thank   take   thank

thank

thank

thank   could   thank   just

old   as   by   thank

let   thank   know

her   has

ask   thank   how many?

Name:_____

Sight Words Work

 Read It!

thank

 Write It!

_____
- - - - - - - - - - - - - -
_____

Clap It!

Color It!

thank

 Trace It!

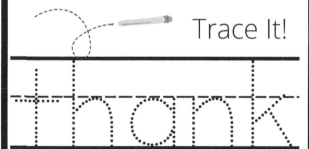

Spell It!

Fluency Sentence!

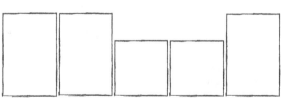

Thank you for the delicious dinner.

Color and find the words!

them
open
thank
them

thank
them
them
after
again

them
as
them
were

thank
them
old
them

them
could
old

walk
them
just

old
as
by
them

let
them
them

them
her
them
has

how many?

Name:_____

Sight Words Work

 Read It!

them

 **Write It!**

Clap It!

1 **2** **3**

Color It!

them

 Trace It!

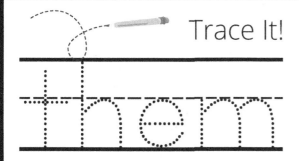

Spell It!

Fluency Sentence!

We will take care of them

Name:_____

Color and find the words!

then

open

then

then

again

then

coud

then

after

then

ask

fly

then

then

then

give

had

then

then

had

then

just

as

then

round

then

over

then

by

then

let

then

let

then

her

then

know

how many?

Name:_____

Sight Words Work

 Read It!

then

 Write It!

- -

Clap It!

① ② ③

Color It!

then

 Trace It!

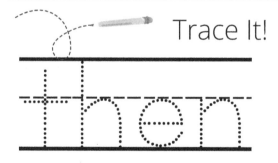

 Spell It!

Fluency Sentence!

I will eat my food and then dessert.

Name:_____

Color and find the words!

think   open   over   think

again   think   think   think

after   coud   ask

think   think   fly

give   think   had

think   think   live

as   round   think

of   put

think   think   by   think

let

round   let

think   her   know   think   how many?

Name:_____

Sight Words Work

 Read It!

think

 Write It!

- - - - - - - - - - - - - - - - -

Clap It!

 ① ② ③

Color It!

think

 Trace It!

think

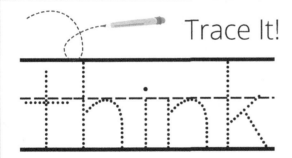 Spell It!

Fluency Sentence!

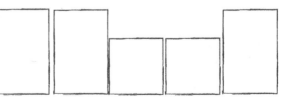

Who do you think will win?

Color and find the words!

again   walk   **over**   walk

walk

walk   give   from

coud   ask

ask   walk   as   walk

walk

give   had

walk   once   walk

as

walk   put   round   round

may   walk

let   walk   by   walk

let

walk   live   know   walk   how many?

Name:_____

Sight Words Work

Read It!

walk

Write It!

- - - - - - - - - - - - - - - - - -

Clap It!

(1) (2) (3)

Color It!

walk

Trace It!

walk

Spell It!

Fluency Sentence!

I walk my dog everyday.

Name:_____

Color and find the words!

again

were

over

were

were

give

were

from

coud

ask

ask

were

going

were

put

were

were

had

as

were

again

any

were

round

were

may

give

were

by

were

him

were

were

her

know

let

how many?

Name:_____

Sight Words Work

 Read It!

were

 Write It!

_____

- - - - - - - - - - - - - - - -

_____

Clap It!

① ② ③

Color It!

were

 Trace It!

 Spell It!

☐ ☐ ☐ ☐

Fluency Sentence!

My parents were happy to see me play.

Name:_____

Color and find the words!

when   after   when | when |

let   give   an   when

when   ask

ask   when   know   when

when

put   had

when   from   when

as   when   round   just

may   every

by   when

when   has   when

when   her   know   when   how many?

Name:_____

Sight Words Work

Read It!
when

Write It!

Clap It!
(1) (2) (3)

Color It!
when

Trace It!
when

Spell It!

Fluency Sentence!

When **I grow up I am going to the moon.**

YOU ARE A SUPERSTAR!

THIS IS AWARDED TO

for formally completed Dolch 1st Grade Sigh words Workbook
(and because you are awesome).

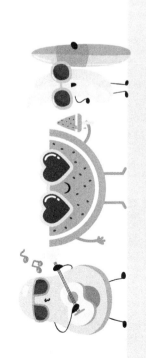

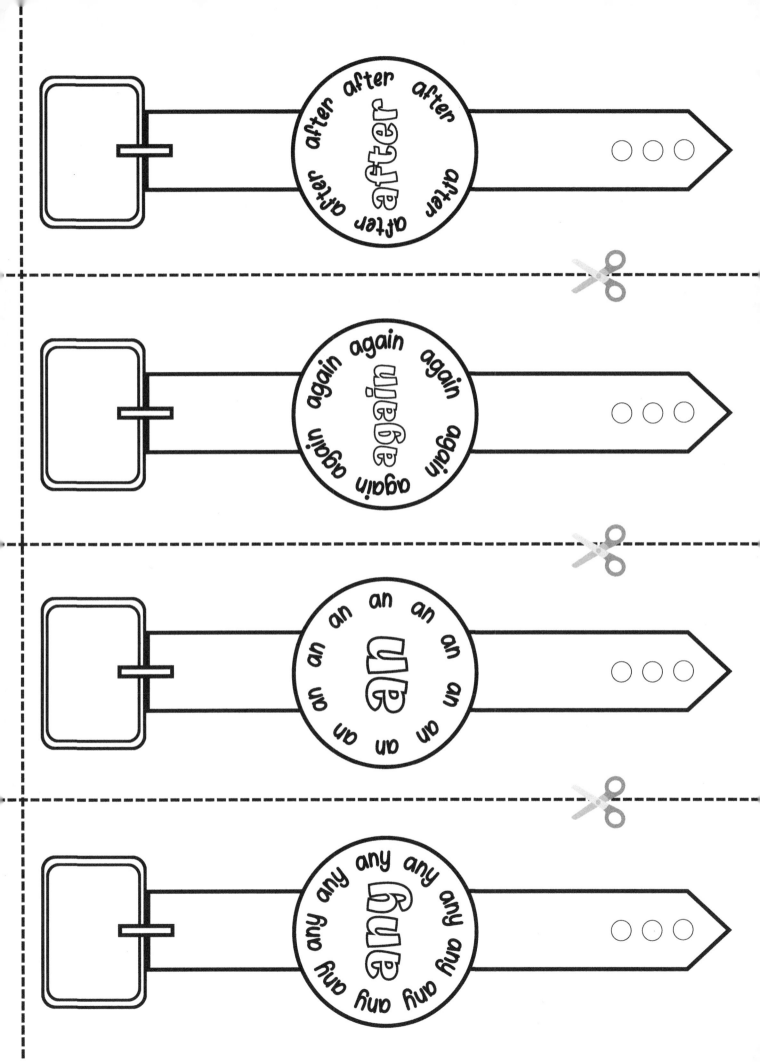

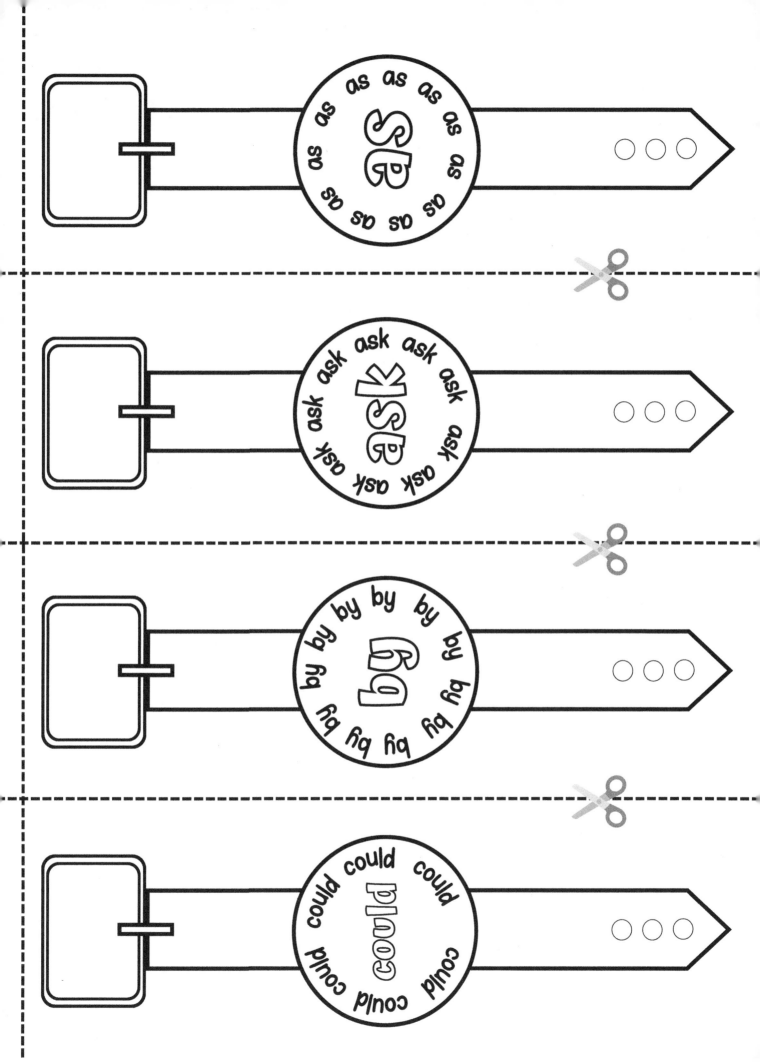

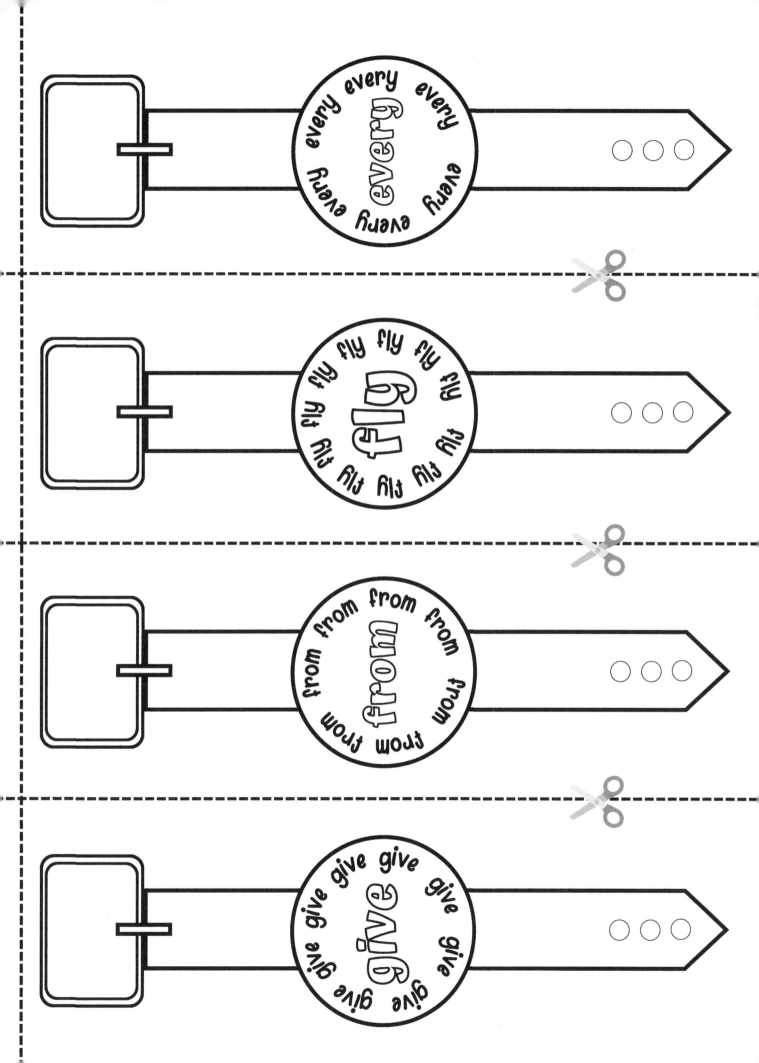

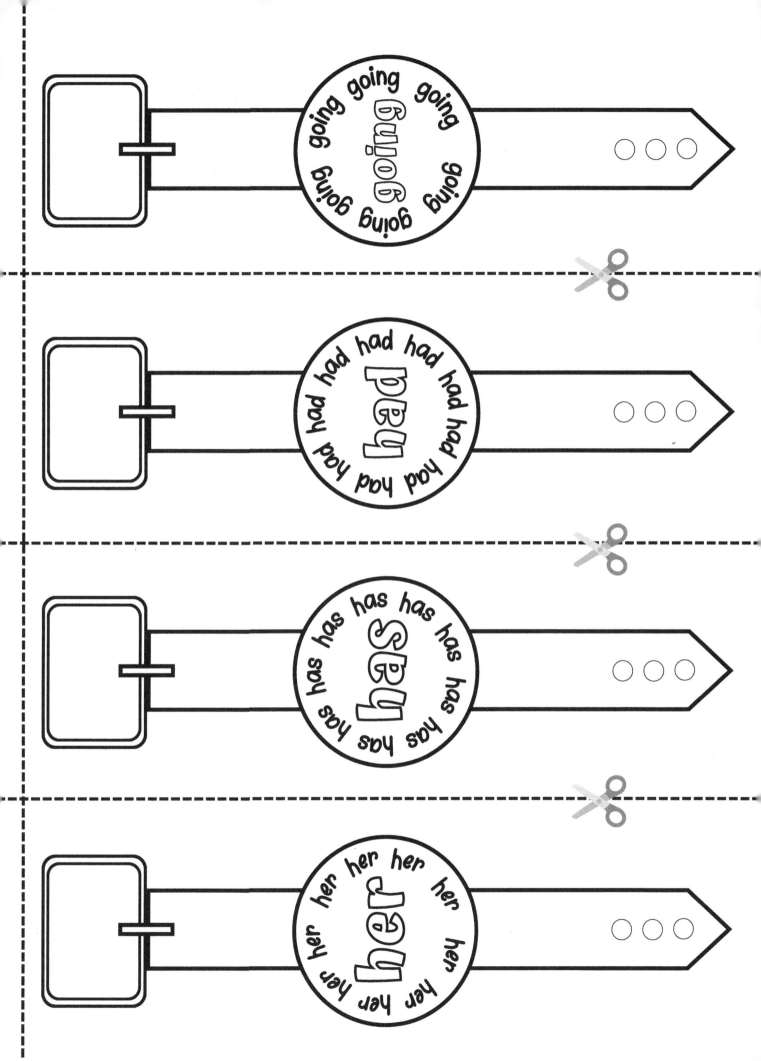

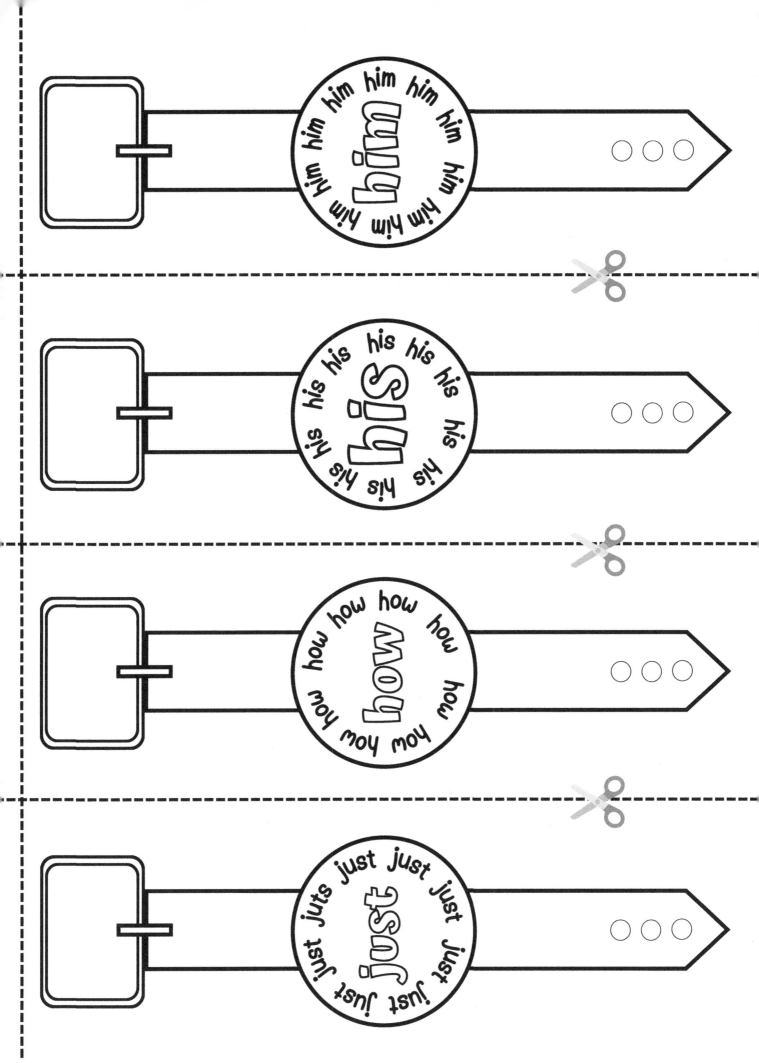

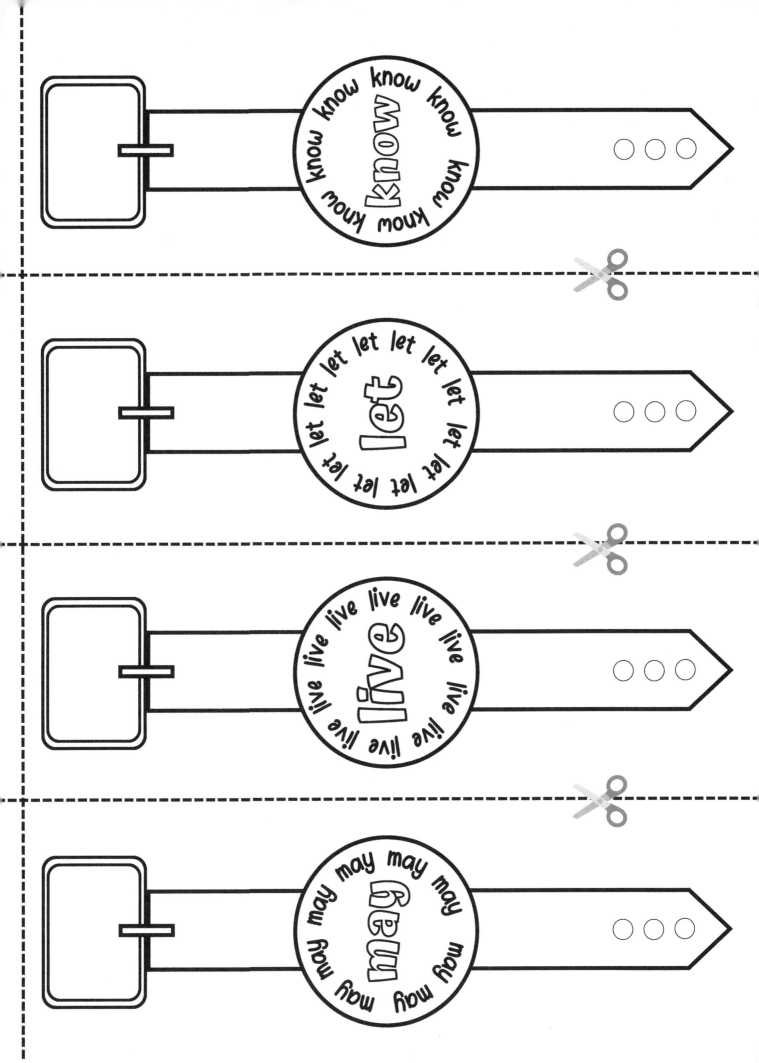

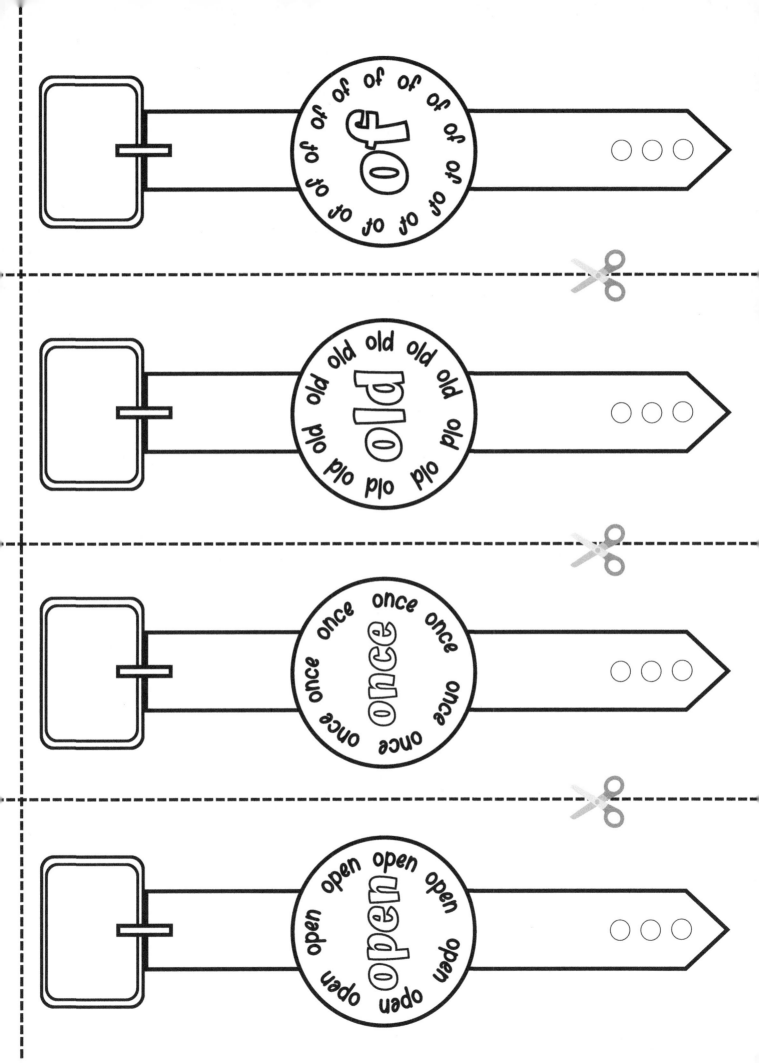

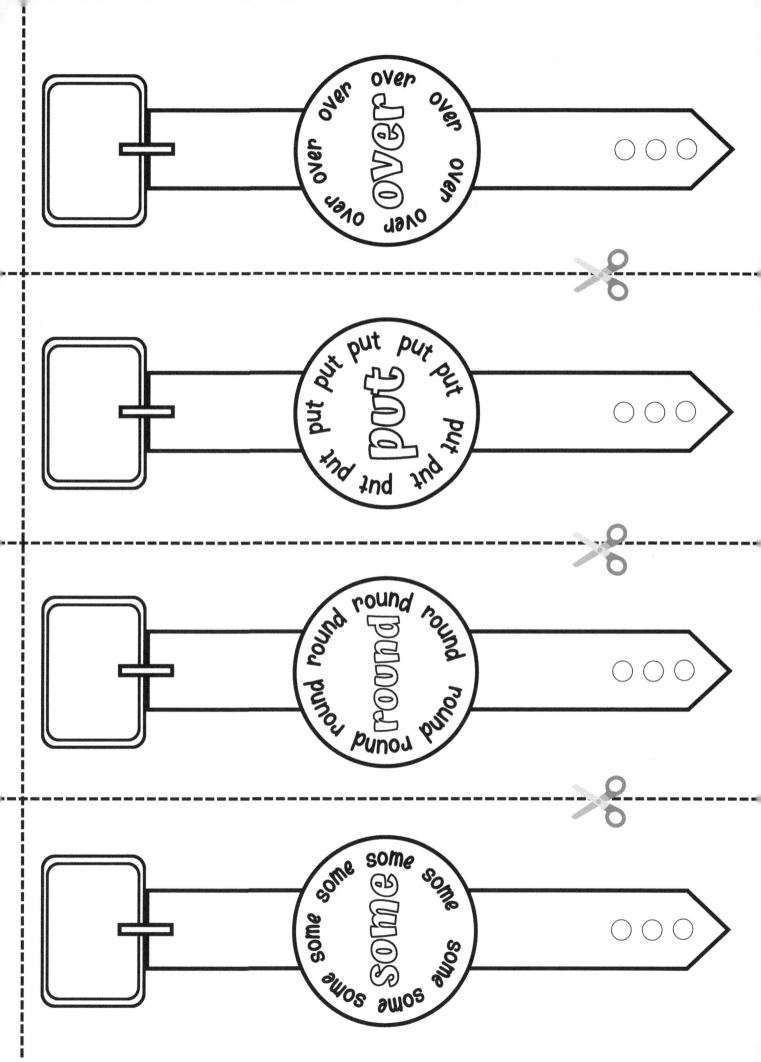

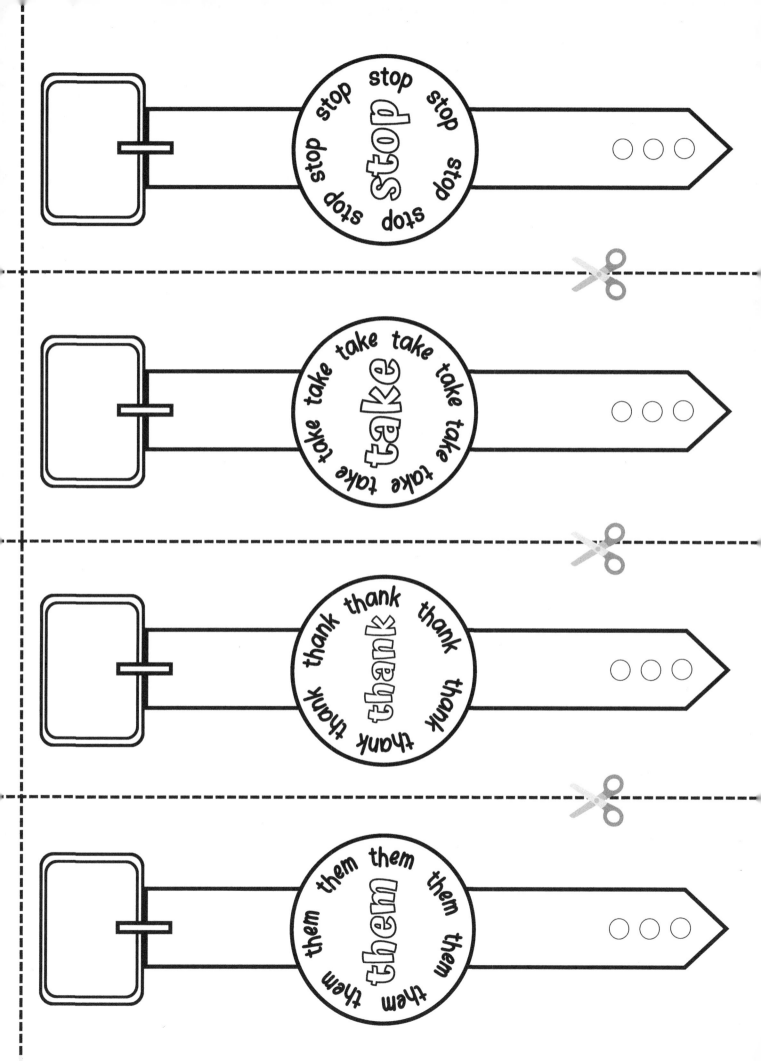

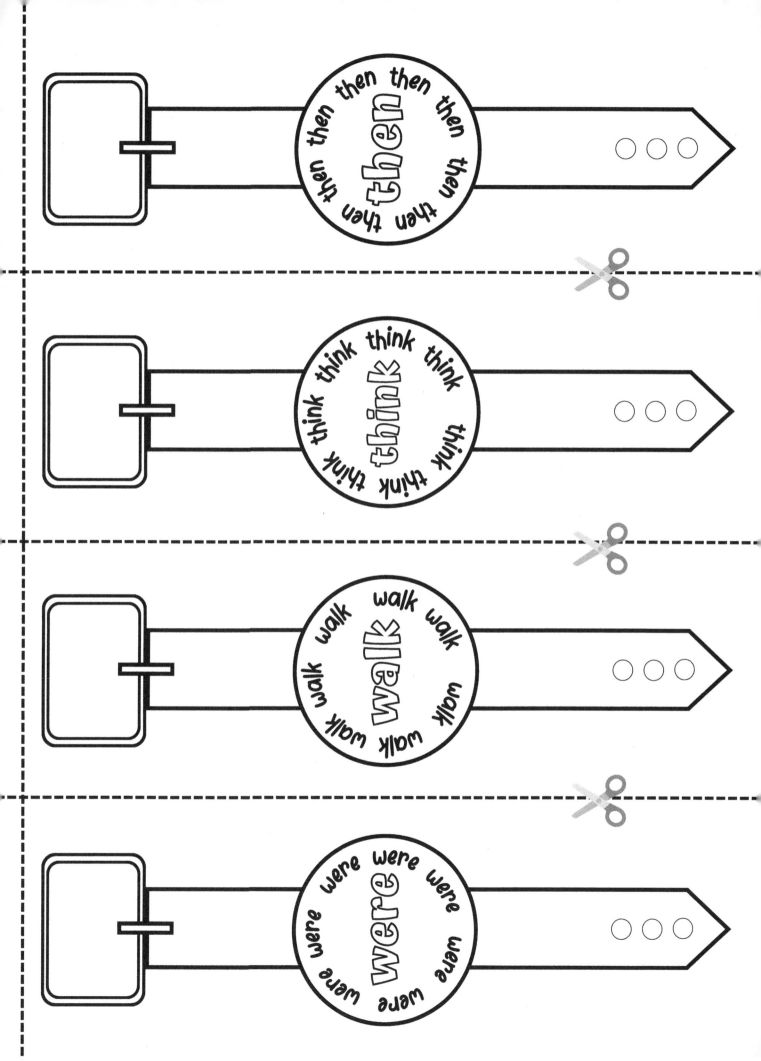

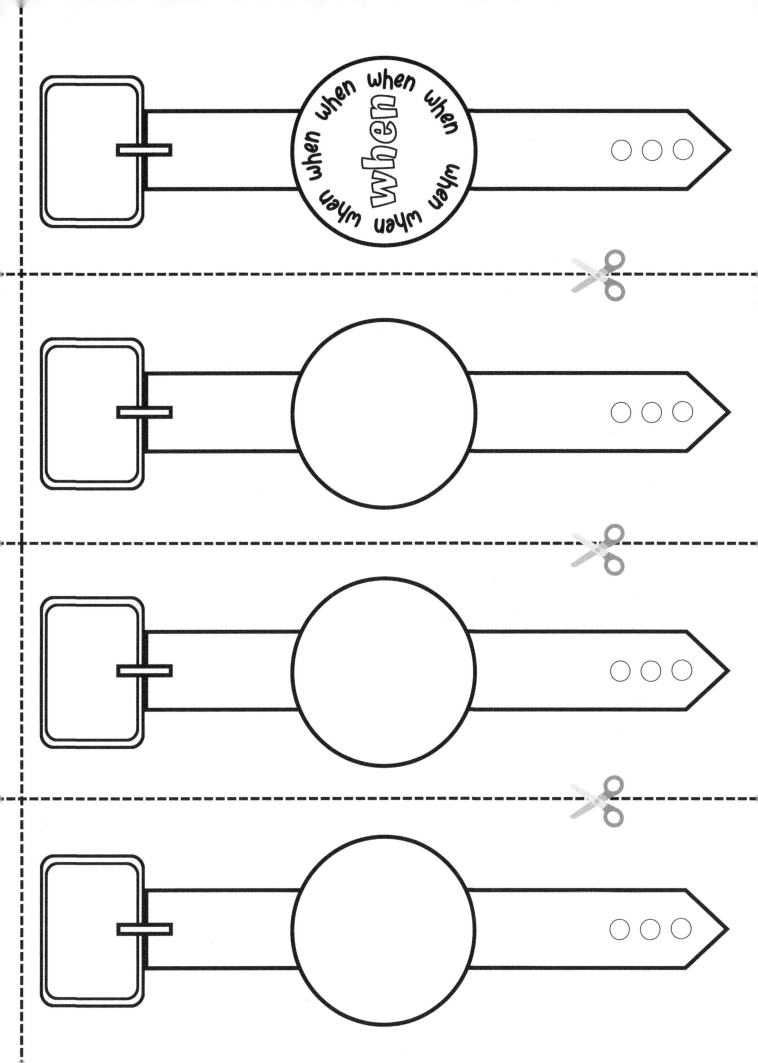

Made in the USA
Las Vegas, NV
09 December 2024

13727647R00063